Frances R. Havergal

Songs of Peace and Joy

Frances R. Havergal

Songs of Peace and Joy

ISBN/EAN: 9783337223670

Printed in Europe, USA, Canada, Australia, Japan

Cover: Foto ©Thomas Meinert / pixelio.de

More available books at **www.hansebooks.com**

Songs of Peace and Joy.

THE MUSIC BY
CHARLES H. PURDAY.

THE WORDS SELECTED FROM

" THE MINISTRY OF SONG " *and* " UNDER THE SURFACE,"

WRITTEN BY

FRANCES RIDLEY HAVERGAL.

SECOND EDITION.

London:

JAMES NISBET & CO., 21, BERNERS STREET, W.

WEEKES & CO., 16, HANOVER STREET, W.

1879.

PREFATORY NOTE.

THIS little book contains upwards of Thirty musical settings of selected verses from

" THE MINISTRY OF SONG " and " UNDER THE SURFACE."

It may be interesting to mention that, with the exception of three or four, they are the production of an octogenarian friend, whose desire is that his work may be to the glory of that faithful God who has led him for more than twice forty years through the wilderness; and that his chosen title for these little melodies,

" SONGS OF PEACE AND JOY,"

may be true of the experience of all who shall sing them.

FRANCES RIDLEY HAVERGAL.

May 13, 1879.

COMPOSER'S PREFACE.

IN publishing this little volume, I desire to say that I had never read any of Miss Havergal's beautiful Poems until the summer of 1878, when I was so charmed with the natural flow, lyrical aptitude, and truly Christian sentiments of her poetry, that I felt an intense desire to set some of her Hymns to music. I accordingly wrote to ask her permission to do so, which she readily and most kindly granted, by a short note to me dated August 10, 1878. I then set three of them, which I sent for her approval— viz., " Ministry of Song," v. 1 and 11, " Be not Weary," and " Wait patiently for Him,"—when she replied, August 24, 1878 : " Some of the Hymns have been set already ; it would save possible disappointment if you would say beforehand which you would like to set. . . . . Your name is so well known to me, and was so honoured by my dear father, that I am specially gratified at your music and my little words being linked together. May our God grant his special blessing on your plan." Thus encouraged, I went on adapting and occasionally sending her my tunes until they had reached about thirty, corresponding with her at intervals, until it became necessary that we should determine how they should be published. This suggested an interview, and an invitation was sent me to go to Wales for the purpose of going through the M.S. together. " Man proposes, but God disposes," and it was ordered otherwise. Consequently a request was made that I should send the M.S. down, as Miss H. said she could look it over then, and return it before she went on her projected tour to her Irish mission. This was done and the M.S. returned with copious notes and valuable suggestions, to which I had much pleasure in giving effect,— when it pleased the Disposer of all events to call her hence,—how gloriously prepared has been fully stated.* And I have reason to bless God for my acquaintance with her and her works.

C. H. P.

Oct. 1, 1879.   * " The Last Week."

INDEX.

Those marked with a star, thus, *, are specially suitable for Congregational Use, or Public Occasions.

Jesus only.

MATT. xvii. 8.

mf

1. 'Je - sus on - ly!' In the sha - dow Of the cloud so
2. 'Je - sus on - ly!' In the glo - ry, When the sha - dows

chill and dim, We are cling - ing, lov - ing, trust - ing,
all are flown, See - ing Him in all His beau - ty.

He with us, and we with Him; All un - seen, though
Sa - tis - fied with Him a - lone; May we join His

ev - er nigh, 'Je - sus on - ly'— all our cry.
ran - somed throng, 'Je - sus on - ly'— all our song.

(7)

Whose I am.

ACTS xxvii. 23.

mf   *cres.*   *mf*

Je - sus, Mas - ter, whose I am, Pur -chased Thine a -

- lone to be, By Thy blood, O spot - less Lamb,

Shed so will - ing - ly for me; Let my heart be

f   *cres.*

all Thine own, Let me live to Thee a - lone.

dim.

(8)

Jesus, Master, whose I am,
  Purchased Thine alone to be,
By Thy blood, O spotless Lamb,
  Shed so willingly for me;
Let my heart be all Thine own,
Let me live to Thee alone.

Other lords have long held sway,
  Now, Thy name alone to bear,
Thy dear voice alone obey,
  Is my daily, hourly prayer.
Whom have I in heaven but Thee?
Nothing else my joy can be.

Jesus, Master! I am Thine;
  Keep me faithful, keep me near;
Let Thy presence in me shine,
  All my homeward way to cheer.
Jesus! at Thy feet I fall,
Oh, be Thou my All-in-All.

Whom I serve.

ACTS xxvii. 23.

Je - sus, Mas - ter, whom I serve, Though so fee - bly
and so ill, Strength - en hand and heart and nerve,
All Thy bid - ding to ful - fil; O - pen Thou mine
eyes to see All the work Thou hast for me.

mf

rall.

(10)

Jesus, Master, whom I serve,
　　Though so feebly and so ill,
Strengthen hand and heart and nerve,
　　All Thy bidding to fulfil;
Open Thou mine eyes to see
All the work Thou hast for me.

Lord, Thou needest not, I know,
　　Service such as I can bring,
Yet I long to prove and show
　　Full allegiance to my King.
Thou an honour* art to me,
Let me be a praise to Thee.

Jesus, Master, wilt Thou use
　　One who owes Thee more than all ?
As thou wilt ! I would not choose,
　　Only let me hear Thy call.
Jesus ! let me always be
In Thy service glad and free.

　　* See marginal reading of 1 Peter iv. 7.

Daily Strength.

DEUT. xxxiii. 25.

mf

'As thy day thy strength shall be,'

This should be e - nough for thee; He who knows thy

frame will spare Bur - dens more than thou canst bear.

'As thy day thy strength shall be,'
This should be enough for thee ;
He who knows thy frame will spare
Burdens more than thou canst bear.

When thy days are veiled in night,
Christ shall give thee heavenly light ;
Seem they wearisome and long,
Yet in Him thou shalt be strong.

Cold and wintry though they prove,
Thine the sunshine of His love ;
Or, with fervid heat oppressed,
In His shadow thou shalt rest.

When thy days on earth are past,
Christ shall call thee home at last,
His redeeming love to praise,
Who hath strengthened all thy days.

Master, say on.

I Sam. iii. 9.

Mas - ter, speak! Thy ser - vant hear - eth, Wait - ing for Thy gra - cious word, Long - ing for Thy voice that cheer - eth; Mas - ter, let it now be heard. I am list -'ning, Lord, for Thee; What hast Thou to say to me?

Master, speak! Thy servant heareth,
  Waiting for Thy gracious word,
Longing for Thy voice that cheereth;
  Master, let it now be heard.
I am listening, Lord, for Thee;
What hast Thou to say to me?

Often through my heart is pealing
  Many another voice than Thine,
Many an unwilled echo stealing
  From the walls of this Thy shrine.
Let Thy longed-for accents fall;
Master, speak! and silence all.

Master, speak! I do not doubt Thee,
  Though so tearfully I plead;
Saviour, Shepherd! oh, without Thee
  Life would be a blank indeed.
But I long for fuller light,
Deeper love, and clearer sight.

Master, speak! I kneel before Thee,
  Listening, longing, waiting still;
Oh! how long shall I implore Thee
  This petition to fulfil!
Hast Thou not one word for me?
Must my prayer unanswered be?

Speak to me by name, O Master,
  Let me *know* it is to me;
Speak, that I may follow faster,
  With a step more firm and free,
Where the Shepherd leads the flock,
In the shadow of the rock!

Master, speak! and make me ready,
  When Thy voice is truly heard,
With obedience, glad and steady,
  Still to follow every word.
I am listening, Lord, for Thee;
Master, speak! oh, speak to me!

(15)

Singing for Jesus.

Ps. xxviii. 7.

Sing - ing for Je - sus, our Sa - viour and King,

Sing - ing for Je - sus, the Lord whom we love;

All a - do - ra - tion we joy - ous - ly bring,

Long - ing to praise as they praise Him a - bove.

(16)

Singing for Jesus, our Saviour and King,
  Singing for Jesus, the Lord whom we love ;
All adoration we joyously bring,
  Longing to praise as they praise Him above.

Singing for Jesus, our Master and Friend,
  Telling His love and His marvellous grace ;
Love from eternity, love to the end,
  Love for the loveless, the sinful and base.

Singing for Jesus, and trying to win
  Many to love Him, and join in the song ;
Calling the weary and wandering in,
  Rolling the chorus of gladness along.

Singing for Jesus, our Life and our Light ;
  Singing for Him as we press to the mark ;
Singing for Him when the morning is bright ;
  Singing, still singing, for Him in the dark.

Singing for Jesus, our Shepherd and Guide,
  Singing for gladness of heart that He gives ;
Singing for wonder and praise that He died,
  Singing for blessing and joy that He lives.

Singing for Jesus, oh, singing for joy !
  Thus will we praise Him and tell out His love,
Till He shall call us to brighter employ,
  Singing for Jesus for ever above.

Not your own.

1 COR. vi. 19.

'Not your own,' but His ye are, Who hath paid a price un - told

For your life, ex-ceed -ing far All earth's store of gems and gold;

With the pre-cious blood of Christ, Ran-som trea-sure all un - priced,

Full re - demp-tion is pro - cured, Full sal - va - tion is as - sured.

'Not your own,' but His ye are,
Who hath paid a price untold
For your life, exceeding far
All earth's store of gems and gold.
With the precious blood of Christ,
Ransom treasure all unpriced,
Full redemption is procured,
Full salvation is assured.

'Not your own,' but His by right,
His peculiar treasure now,
Fair and precious in His sight,
Purchased jewels for His brow!
He will keep what thus He sought,
Safely guard the dearly bought,
Cherish that which He did choose,
Always love, and never lose.

'Not your own,' but His, the King,
His, the Lord of earth and sky,
His, to whom archangels bring
Homage deep and praises high.
What can royal birth bestow?
Or the proudest titles show?
Can such dignity be known
As the glorious name, ' His own'?

'Not your own,' to Him ye owe
All your life and all your love ;
Live, that ye His praise may show,
Who is yet all praise above.
Every day and every hour,
Every gift and every power,
Consecrate to Him alone,
Who hath claimed you for His own.

Teach us, Master, how to give
All we have and are to Thee ;
Grant us, Saviour, while we live,
Wholly, only, Thine to be.
Henceforth be our calling high,
Thee to serve and glorify ;
Ours no longer, but Thine own,
Thine for ever, Thine alone.

Now I see.

JOHN ix. 25.

'Now I see!' But not the part-ing Of the melt-ing earth and sky,

Not a vis-ion dread and startling, Forc-ing one de-spair-ing cry:

But I see the sol-emn say-ing, 'All have sinned, and all must die;

Ho-ly pre-cepts dis-o-bey-ing, Guil-ty all the world must lie.'

(20)

Bend-ing, si-lenced, to the dust, Now I see that God is just.

'Now I see!' But not the parting
   Of the melting earth and sky,
Not a vision dread and startling,
   Forcing one despairing cry :
But I see the solemn saying,
   'All have sinned, and all must die ;
Holy precepts disobeying,
   Guilty all the world must lie.'
Bending, silenced, to the dust,
Now I see that God is just.

'Now I see!' But not the glory,
   Not the face of Him I love,
Not the full and burning story,
   Of the mysteries above :
But I see that God hath spoken,
   How His well-belovèd Son
Kept the laws which man hath broken,
   Died for sins which man hath done.
Dying, rising, throned above !
'Now I see' that God is love.

Be not Weary.

HEB. xii. 2.

mf

Yes! He knows the way is drea-ry, Knows the weak-ness

of our frame, Knows that hand and heart are wea-ry—

He 'in all points' felt the same. He is near to

help and bless; Be not wea-ry, on-ward press.

Yes! He knows the way is dreary,
  Knows the weakness of our frame,
Knows that hand and heart are weary—
  He 'in all points' felt the same.
He is near to help and bless;
Be not weary, onward press.

Look to Him, who once was willing
  All His glory to resign;
That, for thee the law fulfilling,
  All His merit might be thine.
Strive to follow, day by day,
Where His footsteps mark the way.

Look to Him—the Lord of glory—
  Tasting death to win thy life;
Gazing on that 'wondrous story,'
  Canst thou falter in the strife?
Is it not new life to know
That the Lord hath loved thee so?

Look to Him—who ever liveth,
  Interceding for His own;
Seek, yea, claim, the grace He giveth
  Freely from His priestly throne:
Will He not thy strength renew,
With His Spirit's quickening dew?

Look to Him—and faith shall brighten,
  Hope shall soar, and love shall burn,
Peace once more thy heart shall lighten;
  Rise! He calleth thee: return!
Be not weary on thy way;
Jesus is thy strength and stay!

Not yet.

JOHN xiii. 7.

mp

Not yet thou know-est what I do, O fee-ble child of earth,

Whose life is but to an-gel-view The morn-ing of thy birth.

The small-est leaf, the sim-plest flower, The wild bee's ho-ney cell,

slower.

Have les-sons of My love and power Too hard for thee to spell.

Not yet thou knowest what I do.
O feeble child of earth,
Whose life is but to angel-view
The morning of thy birth.
The smallest leaf, the simplest flower,
The wild bee's honey cell,
Have lessons of My love and power
Too hard for thee to spell.

Not yet thou knowest how I bid
Each passing hour entwine
Its grief or joy, its hope or fear,
In one great love-design ;
Nor how I lead thee through the night,
By many a various way,
Still upward to unclouded light,
And onward to the day.

Not yet thou knowest what I do
Within thine own weak breast,
To mould thee to My image true,
And fit thee for My rest.
But yield thee to My loving skill ;
The veilèd work of grace,
From day to day progressing still,
It is not thine to trace.

Yes, walk by faith and not by sight.
Fast clinging to My hand ;
Content to feel My love and might—
Not yet to understand.
A little while thy course pursue,
Till grace to glory grow ;
Then what I am, and what I do,
Hereafter thou shalt know.

Our Saviour and our King.

HEB. ii. 13.

Our Sa-viour and our King, En-throned and crowned a - bove,

Shall with ex - ceed - ing glad-ness bring The chil-dren of His love.

All that the Fa - ther gave, His glo - ry shall be - hold;

Not one whom Je - sus came to save Is miss - ing from His fold.

(26)

Our Saviour and our King,
    Enthroned and crowned above,
Shall with exceeding gladness bring
    The children of His love.
All that the Father gave,
    His glory shall behold ;
Not one whom Jesus came to save
    Is missing from His fold.

He shall confess His own
    From every clime and coast,
Before His Father's glorious throne,
    Before the angel host.
' O righteous Father, see,
    In spotless robes arrayed,
Thy chosen gifts of love to Me,
    Before the worlds were made.

' By new creation Thine,
    By purpose and by grace,
By right of full redemption Mine,
    Faultless before Thy face.
As Thou hast lovèd Me,
    So hast Thou lovèd them ;
Thy precious jewels they shall be,
    My glorious diadem !'

Now, and Afterward.

HEB. xii. 11.

Now, the sow - ing and the weep - ing,

Work - ing hard and wait - ing long;

Af - ter - ward, the gold - en reap - ing,

Har - vest home and grate - ful song.

Now, the sowing and the weeping,
  Working hard and waiting long;
Afterward, the golden reaping,
  Harvest home and grateful song.

Now, the pruning, sharp, unsparing;
  Scattered blossom, bleeding shoot !
Afterward, the plenteous bearing
  Of the Master's pleasant fruit.

Now, the plunge, the briny burden,
  Blind, faint gropings in the sea;
Afterward, the pearly guerdon
  That shall make the diver free.

Now, the long and toilsome duty
  Stone by stone to carve and bring;
Afterward, the perfect beauty
  Of the palace of the King.

Now, the tuning and the tension,
  Wailing minors, discord strong;
Afterward, the grand ascension
  Of the Alleluia song.

Now, the spirit conflict-riven,
  Wounded heart, unequal strife;
Afterward, the triumph given,
  And the victor's crown of life.

Now, the training, strange and lowly,
  Unexplained and tedious now;
Afterward, the service holy,
  And the Master's ' Enter thou !'

The Things that are Behind.

Philip. iii. 13, 14.

mf

Leave be - hind earth's emp - ty plea - sure,

Fleet - ing hope and chang - ing love;

Leave its soon - - cor - ro - ding trea - sure,

There are bet - ter things a - bove.

Leave behind earth's empty pleasure,
  Fleeting hope and changing love ;
Leave its soon-corroding treasure,
  There are better things above.

Leave, oh, leave thy fond aspirings,
  Bid thy restless heart be still ;
Cease, oh, cease thy vain desirings,
  Only seek thy Father's will.

Leave behind thy faithless sorrow,
  And thine every anxious care ;
He who only knows the morrow
  Can for thee its burden bear.

Leave behind the doubting spirit,
  And thy crushing load of sin ;
By thy mighty Saviour's merit,
  Life eternal thou shalt win.

Leave the darkness gathering o'er thee,
  Leave the shadow-land behind ;
Realms of glory lie before thee ;
  Enter in and welcome find.

New Year.

Isa. xli. 10.

mf or f

Stand-ing at the por - tal, Of the op-'ning year, Words of com-fort

meet us, Hush - ing ev - 'ry fear; Spo - ken thro' the si - lence,

cres.

By our Fa-ther's voice, Tender, strong, and faith - ful, Mak-ing us re - joice.

f CHORUS. *2nd time, ff*

On - ward then, and fear not, Chil - dren of the day!

(32)

rall.

For His word shall nev - er, Nev - er pass a - way.

Repeat Chorus, ff

Standing at the portal,
Of the opening year,
Words of comfort meet us,
Hushing every fear;
Spoken through the silence,
By our Father's voice,
Tender, strong, and faithful,
Making us rejoice.
Onward then, and fear not,
Children of the day!
For His word shall never,
Never pass away.

I, the Lord, am with thee,
Be thou not afraid!
I will help and strengthen,
Be thou not dismayed;
Yea, I will uphold thee
With My own right hand,
Thou art called and chosen
In My sight to stand.
Onward then, &c.

For the year before us,
Oh, what rich supplies!
For the poor and needy,
Living streams shall rise;
For the sad and sinful
Shall His grace abound;
For the faint and feeble,
Perfect strength be found.
Onward then, &c.

He will never fail us,
He will not forsake;
His eternal covenant
He will never break!
Resting on His promise,
What have we to fear?
God is all-sufficient
For the coming year!
Onward then, and fear not,
Children of the day!
For His word shall never,
Never pass away.

Hymn to the Holy Spirit.

Tune—"Tryphosa." Feb. x. 15, 23. *Music by* F. R. H.

To Thee, O Com - fort - er Di - vine,

For all Thy grace and power be - nign,

Sing we Al - le - lu - ia!

Al - le - lu - ia! Al - le - lu - ia!

(34)

To Thee, O Comforter Divine,
For all Thy grace and power benign,
  Sing we Alleluia !

To Thee, whose faithful love had place
In God's great Covenant of Grace,
  Sing we Alleluia !

To Thee, whose faithful voice doth win
The wandering from the ways of sin,
  Sing we Alleluia !

To Thee, whose faithful power doth heal,
Enlighten, sanctify, and seal,
  Sing we Alleluia !

To Thee, whose faithful truth is shown
By every promise made our own,
  Sing we Alleluia !

To Thee, our Teacher and our Friend,
Our faithful Leader to the end,
  Sing we Alleluia !

To Thee, by Jesus Christ sent down,
Of all His gifts the sum and crown,
  Sing we Alleluia !

To Thee, who art with God the Son
And God the Father ever One,
  Sing we Alleluia !

Alleluia!

HEB. x. 15, 23.

mf ... *p*

To Thee, O Com-fort-er Di-vine, For all Thy grace and power be-nign,

ff ... *mf*

Sing we Al-le-lu-ia! To Thee, whose faith-ful love had place In

cres. ... *ff*

God's great Co-ve-nant of Grace, Sing we Al-le-lu-ia!

mf ... *rall.*

To Thee, whose faith-ful voice doth win The wan-d'ring from the ways of sin,

(36)

ff tempo.

Sing we Al - le - lu - ia! To Thee, whose faith-ful power doth heal, En -

fff (Full Organ.)

- light - en, sanc - ti - fy, and seal, Sing we Al - le - lu - ia!

To Thee, O Comforter Divine,
For all Thy grace and power benign,
  Sing we Alleluia !
To Thee, whose faithful love had place
In God's great Covenant of Grace,
  Sing we Alleluia !
To Thee, whose faithful voice doth win
The wandering from the ways of sin,
  Sing we Alleluia !
To Thee, whose faithful power doth heal,
Enlighten, sanctify, and seal,
  Sing we Alleluia !

To Thee, whose faithful truth is shown,
By every promise made our own,
  Sing we Alleluia !
To Thee, our Teacher and our Friend,
Our faithful Leader to the end,
  Sing we Alleluia !
To Thee, by Jesus Christ sent down,
Of all His gifts the sum and crown,
  Sing we Alleluia !
To Thee, who art with God the Son
And God the Father ever One,
  Sing we Alleluia !

(37)

Is it for Me?

Cant. i. 7.

Is it for me, dear Sa - viour, Thy glo - ry and Thy rest?

For me, so weak and sin - ful, Oh, shall I thus be blest?

Is it for me to see Thee In all Thy glo - rious grace,

And gaze in end - less rap - ture On Thy be - lov - ed Face?

Is it for me, dear Saviour,
 Thy glory and Thy rest?
For me, so weak and sinful,
 Oh, shall I thus be blest?
Is it for me to see Thee
 In all Thy glorious grace,
And gaze in endless rapture
 On Thy belovèd Face?

Is it for me to listen
 To Thy belovèd Voice,
And hear its sweetest music,
 Bid even me rejoice?
Is it for me, Thy welcome,
 Thy gracious ' Enter in '?
For me, Thy ' Come, ye blessèd !'
 For me, so full of sin?

O Saviour, precious Saviour,
 My heart is at Thy feet,
I bless Thee and I love Thee,
 And Thee I long to meet.
A thrill of solemn gladness
 Has hushed my very heart,
To think that I shall really
 Behold Thee as Thou art;

Behold Thee in Thy beauty,
 Behold Thee face to face;
Behold Thee in Thy glory,
 And reap Thy smile of grace;
And be with Thee for ever,
 And never grieve Thee more!
Dear Saviour, I *must* praise Thee,
 And lovingly adore.

Spirituality of God.

JOHN iv. 24.

What know we, Ho - ly God, of Thee,

Thy be - ing and Thine es - sence pure?

Too bright the ve - ry mys - te - ry

For mor - tal vis - ion to en - dure.

(40)

What know we, Holy God, of Thee,
   Thy being and Thine essence pure ?
Too bright the very mystery
   For mortal vision to endure.

We only know Thy word sublime,
   Thou art a Spirit ! Perfect ! One !
Unlimited by space or time,
   Unknown but through the eternal Son.

By change untouched, by thought untraced,
   And by created eye unseen,
In *Thy great Present* is embraced
   All that shall be, all that hath been.

O Father of our spirits, now
   We seek Thee in our Saviour's face ;
In truth and spirit we would bow,
   And worship where we cannot trace.

Remembrance. (COMMUNION HYMN.)

Cant. ii. 3.

Sit down be - neath His sha - dow, And rest with great de - light;

The faith that now be - holds Him Is pledge of fu - ture sight.

Our Mas-ter's love re - mem - ber, Ex - ceed - ing great and free;

Lift up thy heart in glad - ness, For He re - mem-bers thee.

Sit down beneath His shadow,
  And rest with great delight;
The faith that now beholds Him
  Is pledge of future sight.
Our Master's love remember,
  Exceeding great and free ;
Lift up thy heart in gladness,
  For He remembers thee.

Bring every weary burden,
  Thy sin, thy fear, thy grief ;
He calls the heavy laden
  And gives them kind relief.
His righteousness ' all glorious '
  Thy festal robe shall be ;
And love that passeth knowledge
  His banner over thee.

A little while, though parted,
  Remember, wait, and love,
Until He comes in glory,
  Until we meet above.
Till in the Father's kingdom
  The heavenly feast is spread,
And we behold His beauty,
  Whose blood for us was shed !

Wait Patiently for Him.

Ps. xxxvii. 7.

God doth not bid thee wait, To dis - ap - point at last;

A gold- en pro- mise, fair and great, In pre-cept-mould is cast.

Soon shall the morn - ing gild The dark ho - ri - zon rim,

Thy heart's de - sire shall be ful-filled, 'Wait pa - tient - ly for Him.'

(44)

God doth not bid thee wait,
   To disappoint at last ;
A golden promise, fair and great,
   In precept-mould is cast.
Soon shall the morning gild
   The dark horizon rim,
Thy heart's desire shall be fulfilled,
   ' *Wait* patiently for Him.'

The weary waiting times
   Are but the muffled peals,
Low preluding celestial chimes
   That hail His chariot-wheels.
Trust Him to tune thy voice
   To blend with seraphim ;
His 'Wait' shall issue in 'Rejoice !'
   'Wait *patiently* for Him.'

He doth not bid thee wait,
   Like driftwood on the wave,
For fickle chance or fixèd fate
   To ruin or to save.
Thine eyes shall surely see,
   No distant hope or dim,
The Lord thy God arise for thee :
   'Wait patiently *for Him !*'

The Sovereignty of God.

Ps. xlvi. 10.

God Al- migh- ty! King of na- tions! earth Thy foot-stool, heaven Thy throne!

Thine the great-ness, power, and glo - ry, Thine the king-dom, Lord, a - lone!

Life and death are in Thy keep- ing, and Thy will or - dain - eth all:

From the ar - mies of Thy hea- vens to an un - seen in - sect's fall.

God Almighty! King of nations! earth Thy footstool, heaven Thy throne!

Thine the greatness, power, and glory, Thine the kingdom, Lord, alone!

Life and death are in Thy keeping, and Thy will ordaineth all :

From the armies of Thy heavens to an unseen insect's fall.

Reigning, guiding, all-commanding, ruling myriad worlds of light ;

Now exalting, now abasing, none can stay Thy hand of might !

Working all things by Thy power, by the counsel of Thy will,

Thou art God ! enough to know it, and to hear Thy word : 'Be still !'

In Thy sovereignty rejoicing, we Thy children bow and praise,

For we know that kind and loving, just and true are all Thy ways.

While Thy heart of sovereign mercy, and Thine arm of sovereign might,

For our great and strong salvation in Thy sovereign grace unite.

New Mercies.

REV. xxi. 5.

mf or f

New mer - cies, new bless - ings, new light on thy way;

New cou - rage, new hope, and new strength for each day;

New notes of thanks - giv - ing, new chords of de - light;

rall.

New praise in the morn - ing, new songs in the night;

(48)

New mercies, new blessings, new light on thy way ;

New courage, new hope, and new strength for each day ;

New notes of thanksgiving, new chords of delight ;

New praise in the morning, new songs in the night ;

New wine in thy chalice, new altars to raise ;

New fruit for thy Master, new garments of praise ;

New gifts from His treasures, new smiles from His face ;

New streams from the Fountain of infinite grace ;

New stars for thy crown, and new tokens of love ;

New gleams of the glory that waits thee above ;

New light of His countenance, clear and unpriced !

All this be the joy of thy new life in Christ !

This same Jesus.

ACTS i. 11.

mf

'This same Je-sus!' oh! how sweet-ly Fall those words up - on the ear,

Like a swell of far - off mu - sic In the night-watch still and drear.

He who healed the hope-less le - per, He who dried the wi-dow's tear;

He who changed to health and glad-ness Help-less suf-f'ring, trem-bling fear.

' This same Jesus !' oh ! how sweetly
   Fall those words upon the ear,
Like a swell of far-off music
   In the night-watch still and drear.
He who healed the hopeless leper,
   He who dried the widow's tear ;
He who changed to health and gladness
   Helpless suff'ring, trembling fear.

He who wandered, poor and homeless,
   By the stormy Galilee ;
He who on the night-robed mountain
   Bent in prayer the wearied knee ;
He who spake as none had spoken,
   Angel-wisdom far above,
All-forgiving, ne'er upbraiding,
   Full of tenderness and love.

He who gently called the weary,
   ' Come, and I will give you rest ';
He who loved the little children,
   Took them in His arms and blest ;
He, the lonely Man of Sorrows,
   'Neath our sin-curse bending low ;
By His faithless friends forsaken
   In the darkest hour of woe.

He Himself, and ' not another,'
   He for whom our heart-love yearned
Through long years of twilight waiting,
   To His ransomed ones returned.
For His word, O Lord, we bless Thee,
   Bless our Master's changeless name ;
Yesterday, to-day, for ever,
   Jesus Christ is still the same.

A Worker's Prayer.

ROM. xiv. 7.

Lord, speak to me, that I may speak In
liv - ing e - choes of Thy tone:
As Thou hast sought, so let me seek Thy
er - ring chil - dren, lost and lone.

Lord, speak to me, that I may speak
  In living echoes of Thy tone :
As Thou hast sought, so let me seek
  Thy erring children, lost and lone.

Oh, lead me, Lord, that I may lead
  The wandering and the wavering feet ;
Oh, feed me, Lord, that I may feed
  Thy hungering ones with manna sweet.

Oh, strengthen me, that while I stand
  Firm on the Rock, and strong in Thee,
I may stretch out a loving hand
  To wrestlers with the troubled sea.

Oh, teach me, Lord, that I may teach
  The precious things Thou dost impart ;
And wing my words, that they may reach
  The hidden depths of many a heart.

Oh, give Thine own sweet rest to me,
  That I may speak with soothing power
A word in season, as from Thee,
  To weary ones in needful hour.

Oh, fill me with Thy fulness, Lord,
  Until my very heart o'erflow
In kindling thought and glowing word,
  Thy love to tell, Thy praise to show.

Oh, use me, Lord, use even me,
  Just *as* Thou wilt, and *when*, and *where* ;
Until Thy blessèd Face I see,
  Thy rest, Thy joy, Thy glory share.

Our Commission.

REV. xxii. 17.

Ye who hear the bless - ed call Of the

Spi - rit and the Bride: Hear the Mas - ter's word to all,

Your com - mis - sion and your guide— 'And let

him that hear-eth say, Come,' to all yet far a - way.

Ye who hear the blessèd call
　　Of the Spirit and the Bride:
Hear the Master's word to all,
　　Your commission and your guide—
'And let him that heareth say,
Come,' to all yet far away.

'Come!' alike to age and youth,
　　Tell them of our Friend above,
Of His beauty and His truth,
　　Preciousness and grace and love.
Tell them what you know is true,
Tell them what He is to you.

'Come!' to those who do not care
　　For the Saviour's precious death,
Having not a thought to spare
　　For the gracious words He saith.
Ere the shadows gather deep,
Rouse them from their fatal sleep.

'Come!' to those who, while they hear,
　　Linger, hardly knowing why;
Tell them that the Lord is near,
　　Tell them Jesus passes by.
Call them *now*; oh! do not wait,
Lest to-morrow be too late.

Brothers, sisters, do not wait,
　　Speak for Him who speaks to you!
Wherefore should you hesitate?
　　This is no great thing to do.
Jesus only bids you say,
'Come!' and will you not obey?

Lord! to Thy command we bow,
　　Touch our lips with altar fire;
Let Thy Spirit kindle now
　　Faith, and zeal, and strong desire;
So that henceforth we may be
Fellow-workers, Lord, with Thee!

Joined to Christ.

EPH. i. 22, 23.

mf

Joined to Christ in mys - tic u - nion, We Thy

mem- bers, Thou our Head, Sealed by deep and true com - mu - nion,

Risen with Thee, who once were dead— Sa - viour,

we would hum - bly claim All the power of this Thy name.

Joined to Christ in mystic union,
   We Thy members, Thou our Head,
Sealed by deep and true communion,
   Risen with Thee, who once were dead—
Saviour, we would humbly claim
All the power of this Thy name.

Instant sympathy to brighten
   All their weakness and their woe,
Guiding grace their way to lighten,
   Shall Thy loving members know ;
All their sorrows Thou dost bear,
All Thy gladness they shall share.

Make Thy members every hour
   For Thy blessèd service meet ;
Earnest tongues, and arms of power,
   Skilful hands, and hastening feet,
Ever ready to fulfil
All Thy word and all Thy will.

Everlasting life Thou givest
   Everlasting love to see ;
They shall live because Thou livest,
   And their life is hid with Thee.
Safe Thy members shall be found,
When their glorious Head is crowned !

To Thee.

JOHN vi. 68.

mf

I bring my sins to Thee, The sins I can - not

count, That all may clean-sed be In Thy once o - pened

Fount. I bring them, Sa - viour, all to Thee,

The bur - den is too great for me.

I bring my sins to Thee,
The sins I cannot count,
That all may cleansèd be
In Thy once opened Fount.
I bring them, Saviour, all to Thee,
The burden is too great for me.

My heart to Thee I bring,
The heart I cannot read ;
A faithless, wandering thing,
An evil heart indeed.
I bring it, Saviour, now to Thee,
That fixed and faithful it may be.

To Thee I bring my care,
The care I cannot flee,
Thou wilt not only share,
But bear it all for me.
O loving Saviour, now to Thee
I bring the load that wearies me.

I bring my grief to Thee,
The grief I cannot tell ;
No words shall needed be,
Thou knowest all so well.
I bring the sorrow laid on me,
O suffering Saviour, now to Thee.

My joys to Thee I bring,
The joys Thy love hath given,
That each may be a wing
To lift me nearer heaven.
I bring them, Saviour, all to Thee,
For Thou hast purchased all for me.

My life I bring to Thee,
I would not be my own ;
O Saviour, let me be
Thine ever, Thine alone.
My heart, my life, my all I bring
To Thee, my Saviour and my King !

In Memoriam.

"Hermas."

Words by M. J. WALKER.   Ps. lv. 23.   Music by F. R. H.*

Je - sus, I will trust Thee, trust Thee with my soul;

Guil - ty, lost, and help - less, Thou can'st make me whole.

There is none in hea - ven or on earth like Thee:

Thou hast died for sin - ners— there - fore, Lord, for me.

* The first verse of this Hymn was sung by F. R. H. ten minutes before her glorious departure to "eternal rest"—June 3rd, 1879.

(60)

Jesus, I will trust Thee, trust Thee with my soul ;
Guilty, lost, and helpless, Thou canst make me whole.
There is none in heaven or on earth like Thee :
Thou hast died for sinners—therefore, Lord, for me.

Jesus, I may trust Thee, name of matchless worth
Spoken by the angel at Thy wondrous birth ;
Written, and for ever, on Thy cross of shame,
Sinners read and worship, trusting in that name.

Jesus, I must trust Thee, pondering Thy ways,
Full of love and mercy all Thine earthly days :
Sinners gathered round Thee, lepers sought Thy face—
None too vile or loathsome for a Saviour's grace.

Jesus, I can trust Thee, trust Thy written word,
Though Thy voice of pity I have never heard.
When Thy Spirit teacheth, to my taste how sweet—
Only may I hearken, sitting at Thy feet.

Jesus, I do trust Thee, trust without a doubt :
'Whosoever cometh, Thou wilt not cast out,'
Faithful is Thy promise, precious is Thy blood—
These my soul's salvation, Thou my Saviour God !

Take my Life.

Tune—" Patmos."*   2 Sam. xix. 30.   *Music by* Canon Havergal.

Take my life, and let it be
Con - se - cra - ted, Lord, to Thee.
Take my mo - ments and my days,
Let them flow in cease - less praise.

* This setting of the late Canon Havergal's is included in this collection by F. R. H's. request.

(62)

Take my life, and let it be
Consecrated, Lord, to Thee.
Take my moments and my days,
Let them flow in ceaseless praise.

Take my hands, and let them move
With the impulse of Thy love.
Take my feet, and let them be
Swift and ' beautiful ' for Thee.

Take my voice, and let me sing
Always, only, for my King.
Take my lips, and let them be
Filled with messages from Thee.

Take my silver and my gold,
Not a mite would I withhold.
Take my intellect, and use
Every power as Thou dost choose.

Take my will, and make it Thine !
It shall be no longer mine.
Take my heart, it is Thine own !
It shall be Thy royal throne.

Take my love, my Lord, I pour
At Thy feet its treasure-store.
Take myself, and I will be
Ever, only, all, for Thee.

Trusting.

ISA. xii. 2.

I am trust-ing Thee, Lord Je - sus, Trust - ing on - ly
Thee! Trust-ing Thee for full sal - va - tion, Great and free!

I am trust - ing Thee for par - don, At Thy feet I bow;
For Thy grace and ten - der mer - cy Trust - ing now.

I am trusting Thee, Lord Jesus,
  Trusting only Thee!
Trusting Thee for full salvation,
  Great and free!
I am trusting Thee for pardon,
  At Thy feet I bow;
For Thy grace and tender mercy
  Trusting now.

I am trusting Thee for cleansing
  In the crimson flood;
Trusting Thee to make me holy,
  By Thy blood.
I am trusting Thee to guide me,
  Thou alone shalt lead,
Every day and hour supplying
  All my need.

I am trusting Thee for power;
  Thine can never fail:
Words which Thou Thyself shalt give me
  Must prevail.
I am trusting Thee, Lord Jesus,
  Never let me fall!
I am trusting Thee for ever,
  And for all.

Our King.

O Sa-viour, pre-cious Sa-viour, Whom yet un-seen we love,

O Name of might and fa-vour, All o-ther names a-bove:

We wor-ship Thee, we bless Thee, To Thee a-lone we sing;

We praise Thee, and con-fess Thee Our ho-ly Lord and King!

* This setting also of Canon Havergal's to these words is included by F. R. H's. express desire.

O Saviour, precious Saviour,
  Whom yet unseen we love,
O Name of might and favour,
  All other names above :
    We worship Thee, we bless Thee,
      To Thee alone we sing ;
    We praise Thee, and confess Thee
      Our holy Lord and King !

O Bringer of salvation,
  Who wondrously hast wrought,
Thyself the revelation
  Of love beyond our thought :
    We worship Thee, we bless Thee,
      To Thee alone we sing ;
    We praise Thee, and confess Thee
      Our gracious Lord and King !

In Thee all fulness dwelleth,
  All grace and power divine ;
The glory that excelleth,
  O Son of God, is Thine :
    We worship Thee, we bless Thee,
      To Thee alone we sing ;
    We praise Thee, and confess Thee
      Our glorious Lord and King !

Oh, grant the consummation
  Of this our song above,
In endless adoration,
  And everlasting love :
    Then shall we praise and bless Thee,
      Where perfect praises ring,
    And evermore confess Thee
      Our Saviour and our King !

A Question to All.

Ps. li. 15.

mf

Have you not a word for Je-sus? not a word to say for Him?

He is list-'ning thro' the cho-rus of the burn-ing se - ra - phim!

He is list-'ning: does He hear you speak-ing of the things of earth,

On - ly of its pass-ing plea-sure, sel - fish sor-row, emp-ty mirth?

(68)

Part I.

Have you not a word for Jesus? not a word to say for Him?
He is listening through the chorus of the burning seraphim!
He is listening: does He hear you speaking of the things of earth,
Only of its passing pleasure, selfish sorrow, empty mirth?

He has spoken words of blessing, pardon, peace, and love to you,
Glorious hopes and gracious comfort, strong and tender, sweet and true;
Does He hear you telling others something of His love untold,
Overflowings of thanksgiving for His mercies manifold?

Have you not a word for Jesus? Will the world His praise proclaim?
Who shall speak if ye are silent, ye who know and love His name?
You, whom He hath called and chosen His own witnesses to be,
Will you tell your gracious Master, ' Lord, we cannot speak for Thee !'

' Cannot !' though He suffered for you, died because He loved you so !
' Cannot !' though He has forgiven, making scarlet white as snow !
' Cannot !' though His grace abounding is your freely promised aid !
' Cannot !' though He stands beside you, though He says, ' Be not afraid !'

.   .   .   .

What shall be our word for Jesus? Master, give it day by day,
Ever as the need arises, teach Thy children what to say.
Give us holy love and patience, grant us deep humility,
That of self we may be emptied, and our hearts be full of Thee.

Part II.

Yes, we have a word for Jesus ! Living echoes we will be
Of Thine own sweet words of blessing, of Thy gracious ' Come to Me !'
Jesus, Master ! yes, we love Thee ! and to prove our love would lay
Fruit of lips which Thou wilt open, at Thy blessèd feet to-day.

Give us grace to follow fully, vanquishing our faithless shame,
Feebly it may be, but truly, witnessing for Thy dear name.
Ours shall be the joy and honour Thy redeemèd ones to bring,
Jewels for the coronation of our coming Lord and King.

Yes, we have a word for Jesus ! We will bravely speak for Thee ;
And Thy bold and faithful soldiers, Saviour, we would henceforth be ;
In Thy name set up our banners, while Thine own shall wave above,
With Thy crimson Name of Mercy, and Thy golden Name of Love.

Help us lovingly to labour, looking for Thy present smile,
Looking for Thy promised blessing, through the brightening ' little while.'
Words for Thee in weakness spoken Thou wilt here accept and own,
And confess them in Thy glory, when we see Thee on Thy throne.

The Ministry of Song.*

PROV. x. 16; I COR. xiv. 15.

In God's great field of la - bour All work is not the same;

He hath a ser - vice for each one Who loves His ho - ly name;

And you to whom the se - crets Of all sweet sounds are known,

Rise up! for He hath called you To a mis - sion of your own.

* Suitable for " Services of Song.'   (70)

And right - ly to ful - fil it His grace will make you strong,

Who to your charge hath gi - ven The min - is - try of song.

In God's great field of labour
  All work is not the same ;
He hath a service for each one
  Who loves His holy name ;
And you to whom the secrets
  Of all sweet sounds are known,
Rise up ! for He hath called you
  To a mission of your own.
And rightly to fulfil it
  His grace will make you strong,
Who to your charge hath given
  The ministry of song.

Sing on in grateful gladness,
  Rejoice in this good thing,
Which the Lord thy God hath given
    to thee :
  The happy power to sing ;
But yield to Him, the Sovereign
  To whom all gifts belong,
In fullest consecration,
  Your ministry of song ;
Until His mercy grant you
  That resurrection voice,
Whose only ministry shall be
  To praise Him and rejoice.

(71)

Thee Alone.

JOHN xv. 5.

I could not do with-out Thee, O Sa-viour of the lost!

Whose pre-cious blood re-deemed me At such tre-men-dous cost.

Thy righ-teous-ness, Thy par - don, Thy pre-cious blood must be

My on - ly hope and com - fort, My glo - ry and my plea.

I could not do without Thee,
O Saviour of the lost !
Whose precious blood redeemed me
At such tremendous cost.
Thy righteousness, Thy pardon,
Thy precious blood must be
My only hope and comfort,
My glory and my plea.

I could not do without Thee!
I cannot stand alone ;
I have no strength or goodness,
No wisdom of my own.
But Thou, belovèd Saviour,
Art all in all to me ;
And weakness will be power,
If leaning hard on Thee.

I could not do without Thee !
For oh ! the way is long,
And I am often weary,
And sigh replaces song.
How *could* I do without Thee ?
I do not know the way ;
Thou knowest and Thou leadest,
And wilt not let me stray.

I could not do without Thee,
O Jesus, Saviour dear !
E'en when my eyes are holden,
I know that Thou art near.
How dreary and how lonely
This changeful life would be,
Without the sweet communion,
The secret rest with Thee.

I could not do without Thee !
No other friend can read
The spirit's strange deep longings,
Interpreting its need.
No human heart could enter
Each dim recess of mine,
And soothe and hush and calm it,
O blessed Lord, but Thine !

I could not do without Thee !
For years are fleeting fast,
And soon, in solemn loneliness,
The river must be passed.
But Thou wilt never leave me,
And though the waves roll high,
I know Thou wilt be near me,
And whisper, ' It is I.'

Second Advent.

2 THESS. ii. 1.

Thou art com-ing, O my Sa-viour! Thou art com-ing, O my King!

In Thy beau-ty all - resplendent, In Thy glo-ry all-transcendent; Well may we re -

- joice and sing! Com-ing! In the op-'ning east, Her-ald brightness slow-ly swells!

Com-ing! O my glo-rious Priest, Hear we not Thy gold-en bells?

(74)

Thou art coming, O my Saviour !
Thou art coming, O my King !
In Thy beauty all-resplendent,
In Thy glory all-transcendent ;
 Well may we rejoice and sing !
Coming ! In the opening east,
 Herald brightness slowly swells !
Coming ! O my glorious Priest,
 Hear we not Thy golden bells ?

Thou art coming ! Thou art coming !
 We shall meet Thee on Thy way,
We shall see Thee, we shall know
 Thee,   [Thee
We shall bless Thee, we shall show
 All our hearts could never say !
What an anthem that will be,
 Ringing out our love to Thee,
Pouring out our rapture sweet
 At Thine own all-glorious feet !

Thou art coming ! Rays of glory
 Through the veil Thy death has
 rent,
Touch the mountain and the river
With a golden, glowing quiver,
 Thrill of light and music blent.
Earth is brightened when this gleam
 Falls on flower, and rock, and
 stream ;
Life is brightened when this ray
 Falls upon its darkest day.

Thou art coming ! We are waiting
 With a hope that cannot fail ;
Asking not the day or hour,
Resting on Thy word of power
 Anchored safe within the veil.

Time appointed may be long,
 But the vision must be sure :
Certainty shall make us strong,
 Joyful patience can endure !

Oh the joy to see Thee reigning,
 Thee, my own belovèd Lord !
Every tongue Thy name confessing,
Worship, honour, glory, blessing,
 Brought to Thee with glad ac-
 cord !
Thee, my Master and my Friend,
 Vindicated and enthroned ;
Unto earth's remotest end
 Glorified, adored, and owned !

Not a cloud and not a shadow,
 Not a mist and not a tear,
Not a sin and not a sorrow,
Not a dim and veiled to-morrow,
 For that sunrise grand and clear !
Jesus, Saviour, once with Thee.
 Nothing else seems worth a
 thought !
Oh how marvellous will be
 All the bliss Thy pain hath bought

Thou art coming ! At Thy table
 We are witnesses for this,
While remembering hearts Thou
 meetest,
In communion clearest, sweetest,
 Earnest of our coming bliss.
Showing not Thy death alone,
 And Thy love exceeding great,
But Thy coming and Thy throne,
 All for which we long and wait.

Birthday or Anniversary.

EXOD. iii. 12.

mp or mf

'Cer - tain - ly I will be with thee!' Fa - ther, I have found it true:

To Thy faith-ful-ness and mer - cy I would set my seal a - new.

All the year Thy grace hath kept me, Thou my help in-deed hast been,

Mar - vel - lous the lov-ing-kind-ness ev -'ry day and hour hath seen.

'Certainly I will be with thee!' Father, I have found it true :
To Thy faithfulness and mercy I would set my seal anew.
All the year Thy grace hath kept me, Thou my help indeed hast been,
Marvellous the lovingkindness every day and hour hath seen.

'Certainly I will be with thee!' Let me feel it, Saviour dear,
Let me know that Thou art with me, very precious, very near.
On this day of solemn pausing, with Thyself all longing still,
Let Thy pardon, let Thy presence, let Thy peace my spirit fill.

'Certainly I will be with thee!' Blessèd Spirit, come to me,
Rest upon me, dwell within me, let my heart Thy temple be ;
Through the trackless year before me, Holy One, with me abide !
Teach me, comfort me, and calm me, be my ever-present Guide.

'Certainly I will be with thee!' Starry promise in the night !
All uncertainties, like shadows, flee away before its light.
'Certainly I will be with thee!' He hath spoken : I have heard !
True of old, and true this moment, I will trust Jehovah's word.

BY THE SAME AUTHOR.

Post 4to, in extra cloth gilt, 12s. Bound by Burn.

LIFE MOSAIC : "The Ministry of Song" and "Under the Surface" in one volume. By FRANCES R. HAVERGAL. With twelve illustrations of Alpine scenery and flowers, by the Baroness HELGA VON CRAMM. Printed, in colours, under the superintendence of the Artist, by KAUFMANN, of Baden.

Foolscap 4to, 3s. cloth, gilt edges, or in paper covers, 1s. 6d.

SONGS OF PEACE AND JOY. The Words selected from "The Ministry of Song," and "Under the Surface." By FRANCES RIDLEY HAVERGAL. The Music by CHARLES H. PURDAY.

Royal 32mo, 1s. 6d. cloth, gilt edges.

THE MINISTRY OF SONG.

Crown 8vo, 5s. cloth ; also Cheap Edition, royal 32mo, gilt edges, 1s. 6d. cloth.

UNDER THE SURFACE, and other Poems.

Small Crown 8vo, 3s. 6d. cloth ; also Cheap Editions, 1s. sewed, and 1s. 6d. cloth limp.

BRUEY. A Little Worker for Christ.

Royal 16mo, 1s. cloth.

THE FOUR HAPPY DAYS.

LONDON : JAMES NISBET & CO., 21, BERNERS STREET.

Just published, demy 8vo, 1s.

FRANCES RIDLEY HAVERGAL MEMORIAL CARD. Designed by the Baroness HELGA VON CRAMM, and exquisitely printed in Oil Colours by KAUFMANN, of Baden.

Imperial 32mo, 2d. sewed, 6d. cloth.

MEMORIAL of THE LATE FRANCES RIDLEY HAVERGAL.
" The Last Week."

HAVERGAL'S PSALMODY AND CENTURY OF CHANTS.

A. 6s. 6d.   D.   3s. 6d.

Without Chants.   B. 5s.   E.   3s.   Paper Covers, 2s. 3d.

Four Additional Tunes (Nos. 254—257).   Price 2d.

A Selection of 100 Tunes from the above, suited to Mission Services and Children's Songs of Grace and Glory. Price 4d. Cloth limp, 6d.

N.B.—A valuable Appendix, of 69 Hymns, suited to the special requirements of the present day, may be had bound up with any of the above, for 6d. extra, except P, with which it will be 3d. extra, and F, G, N, and O, with which it will be 4d. extra.

LONDON : JAMES NISBET & CO., 21, BERNERS STREET.

www.ingramcontent.com/pod-product-compliance
Lightning Source LLC
Chambersburg PA
CBHW021521270326
41930CB00008B/1035

*9 7 8 3 3 3 7 2 2 3 6 7 0 *